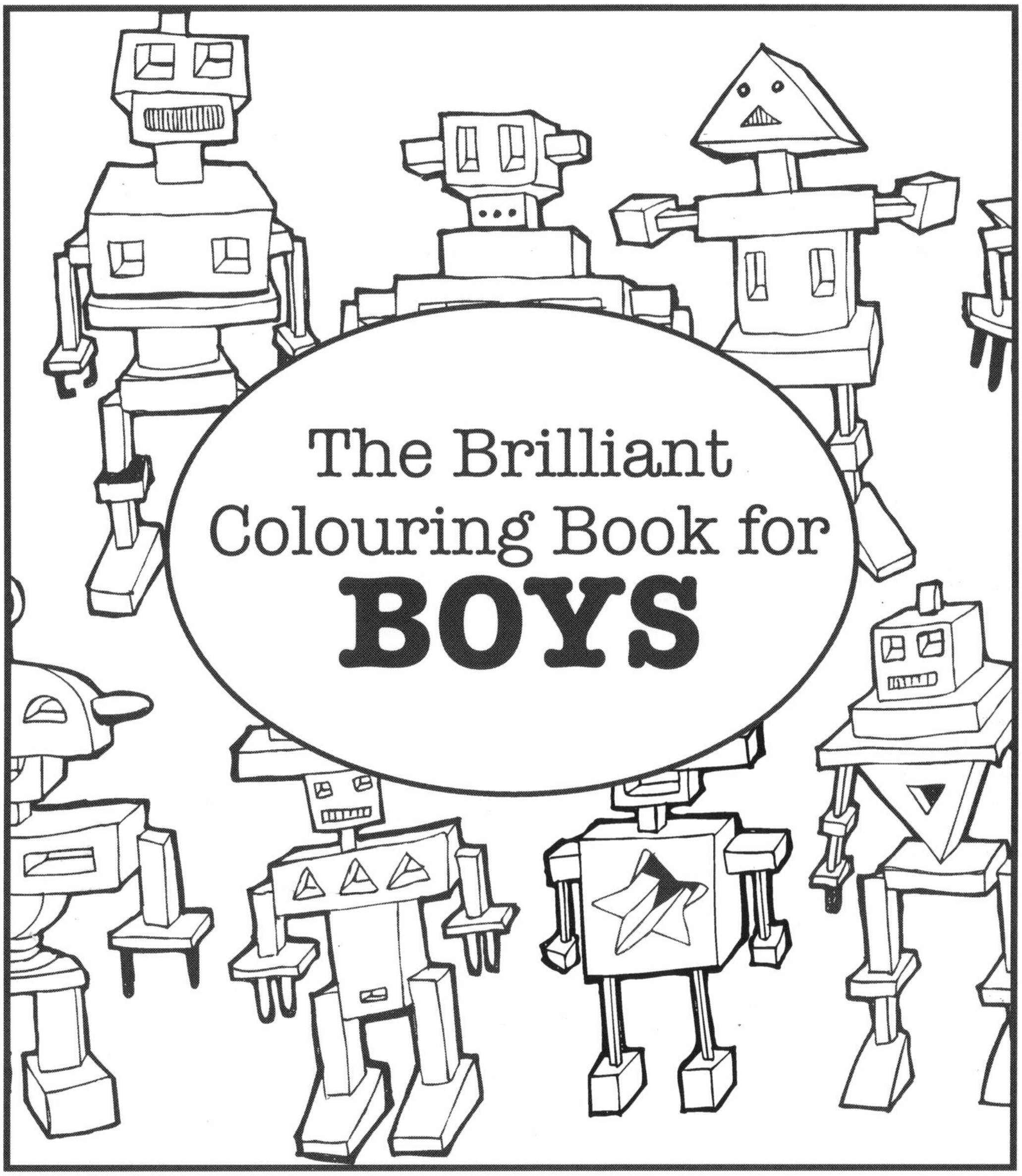

Really **Relaxing** Colouring Book

First published in 2015 by Kyle Craig Publishing

Editor: Alison McNicol

Cover Design: Julie Anson

ISBN: 978-1-908707-96-3

A CIP record for this book is available from the British Library.

A Kyle Craig Publication

www.kyle-craig.com

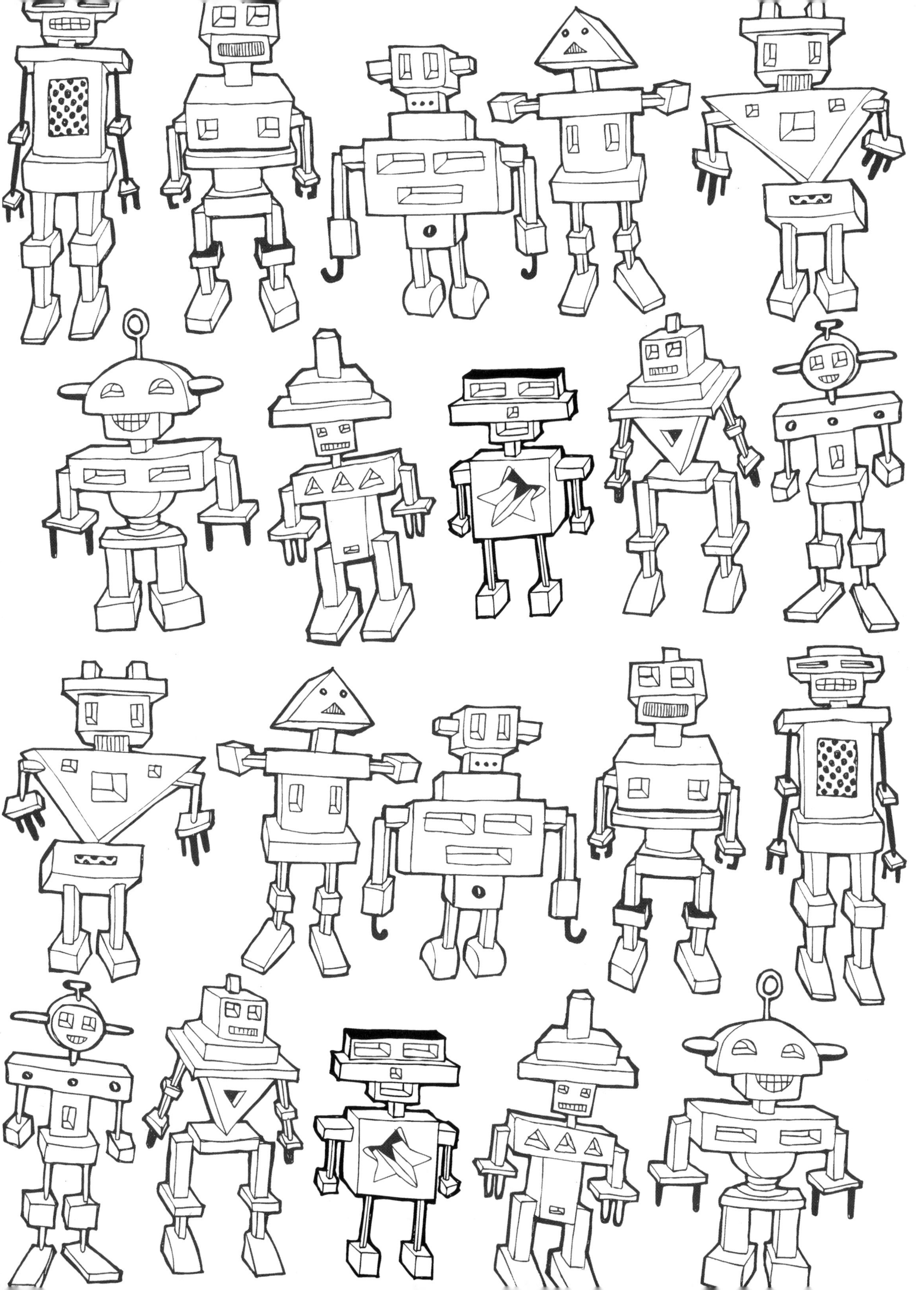

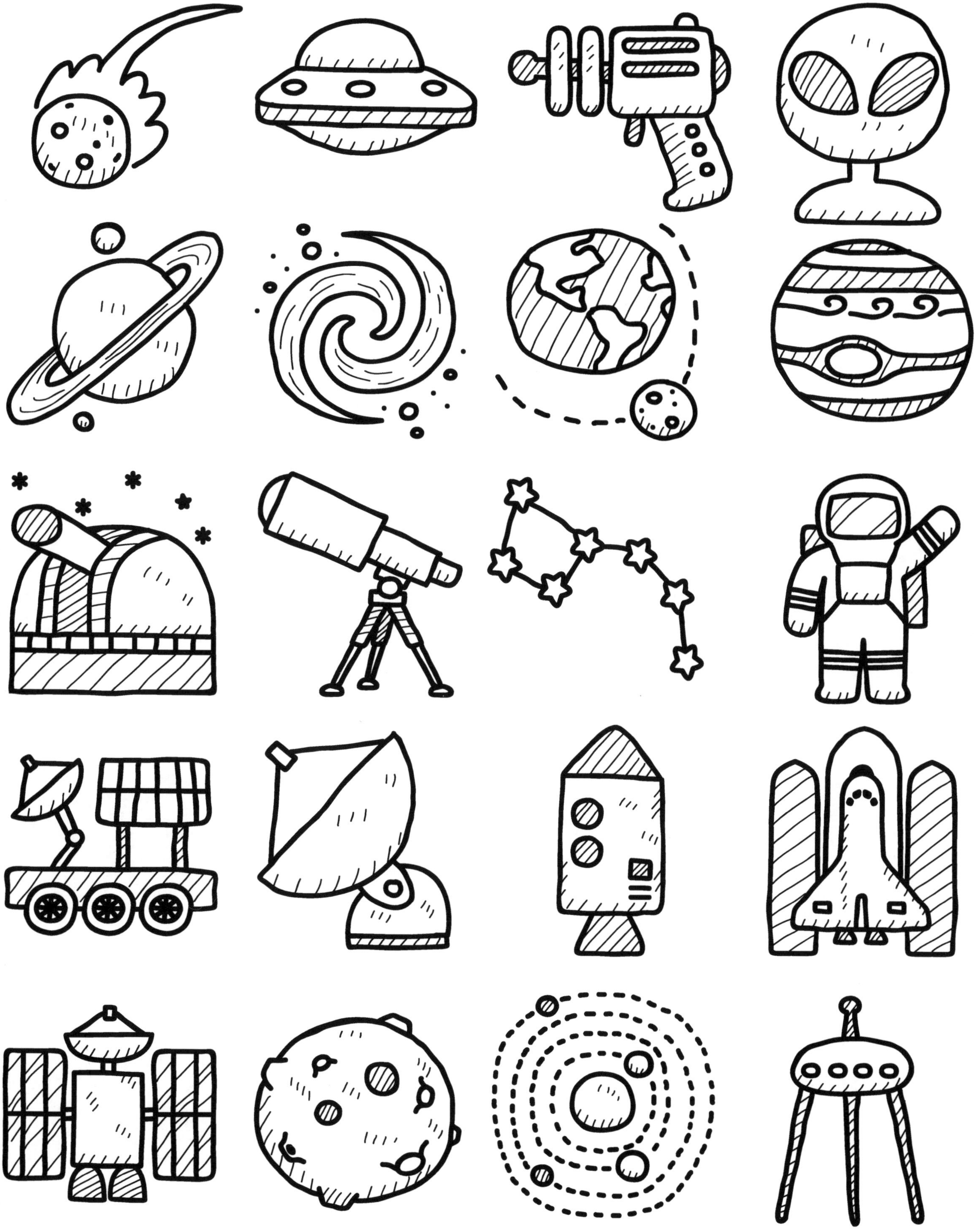

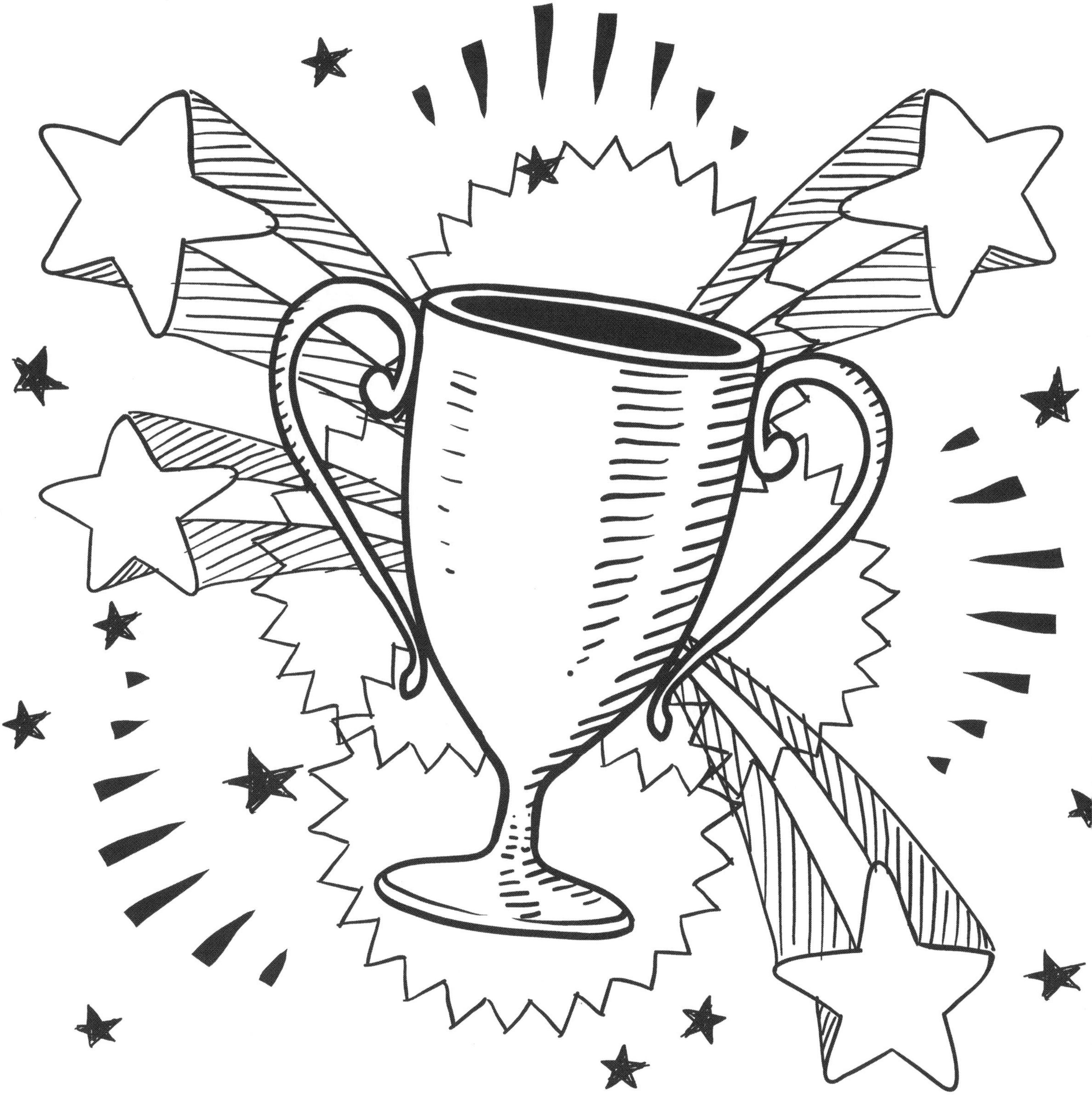

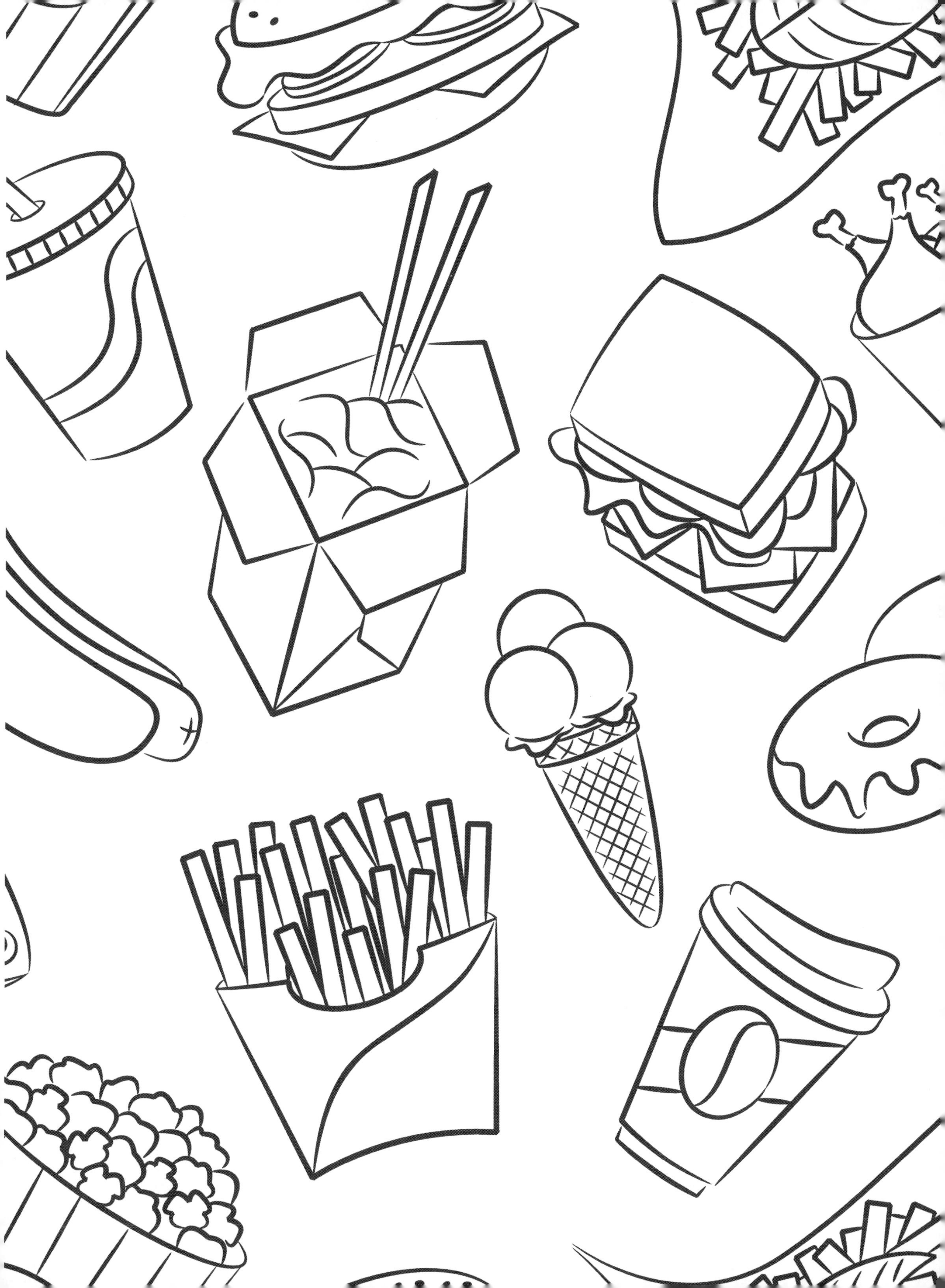

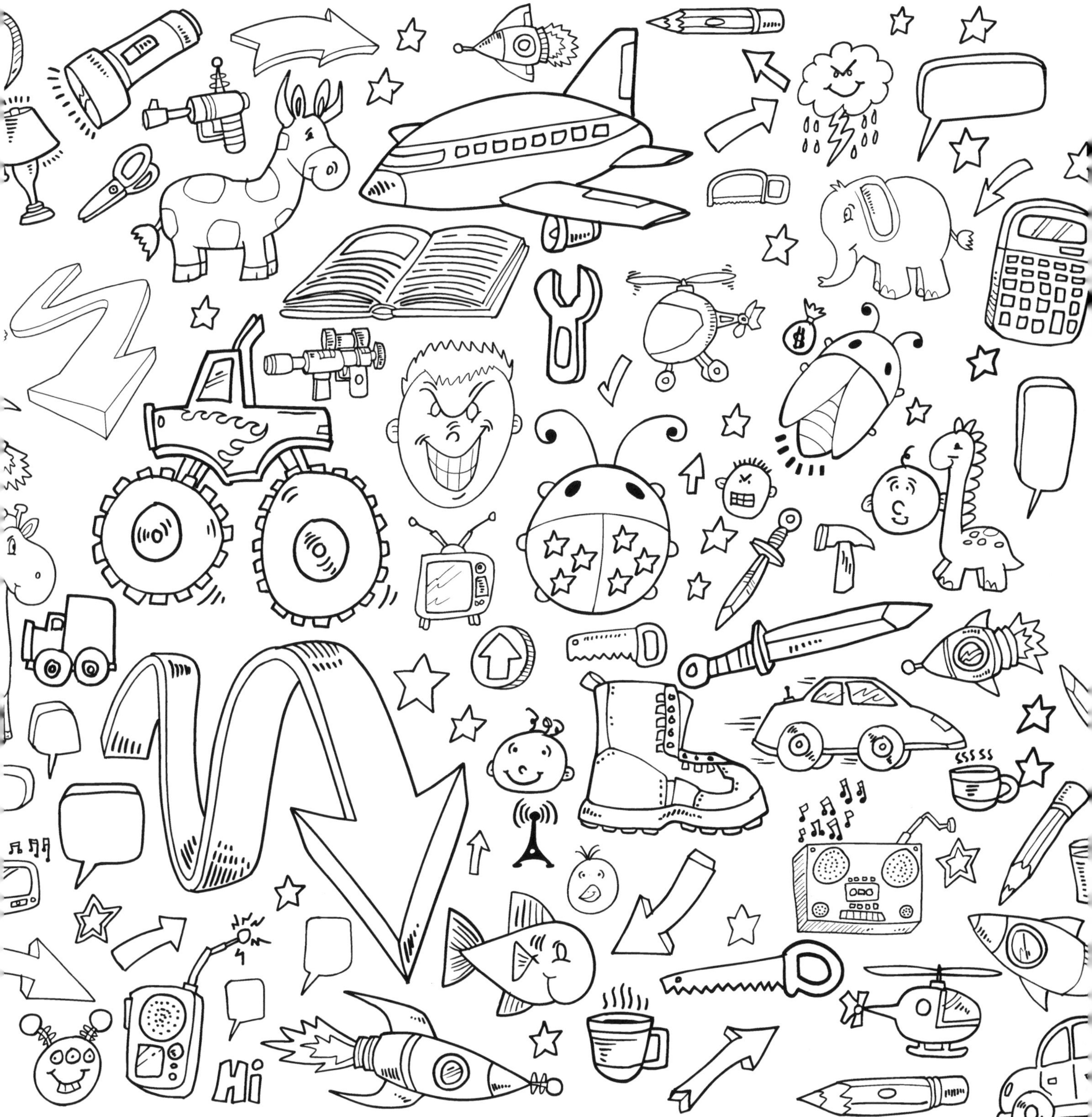
Hi

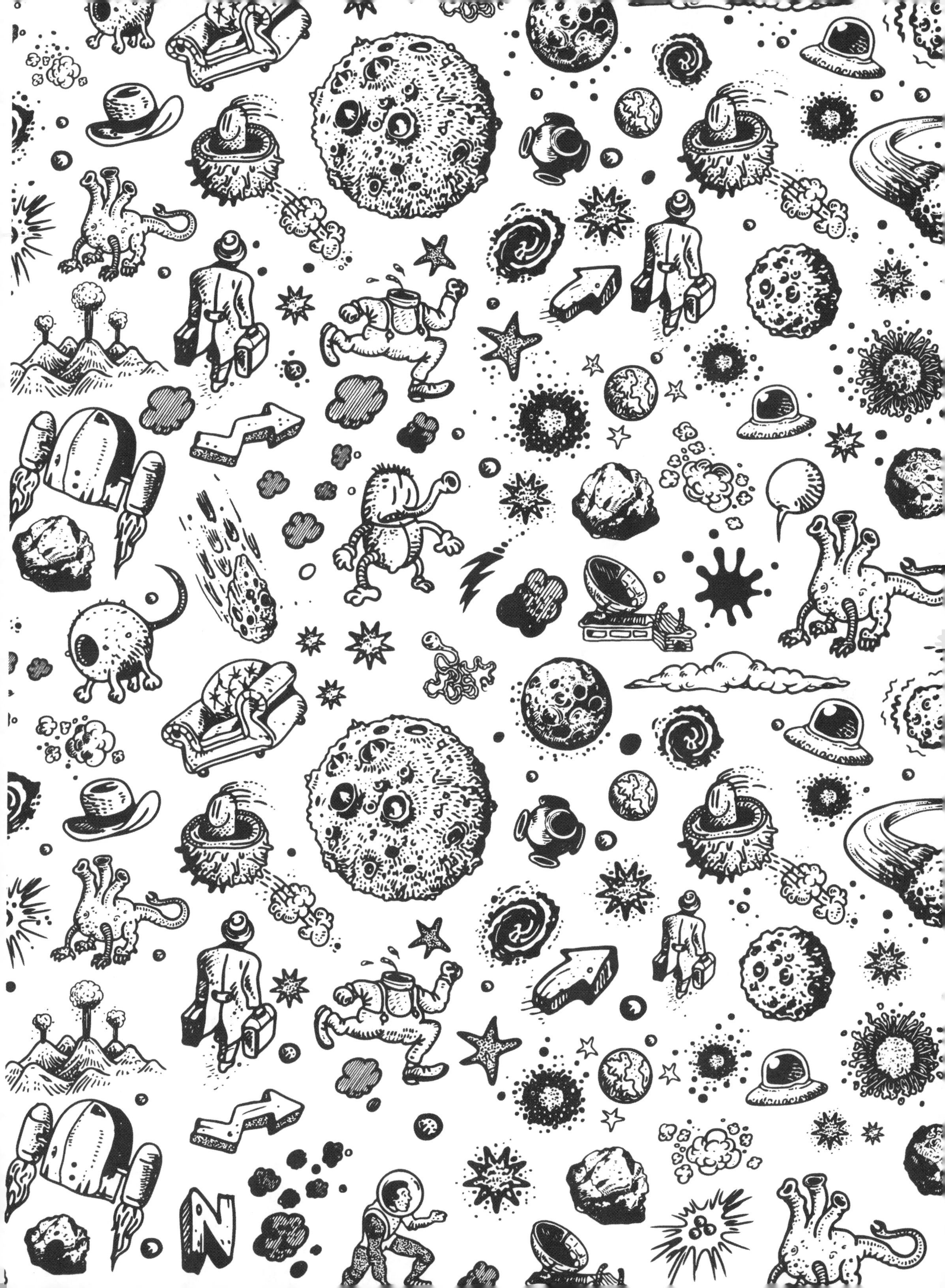
N

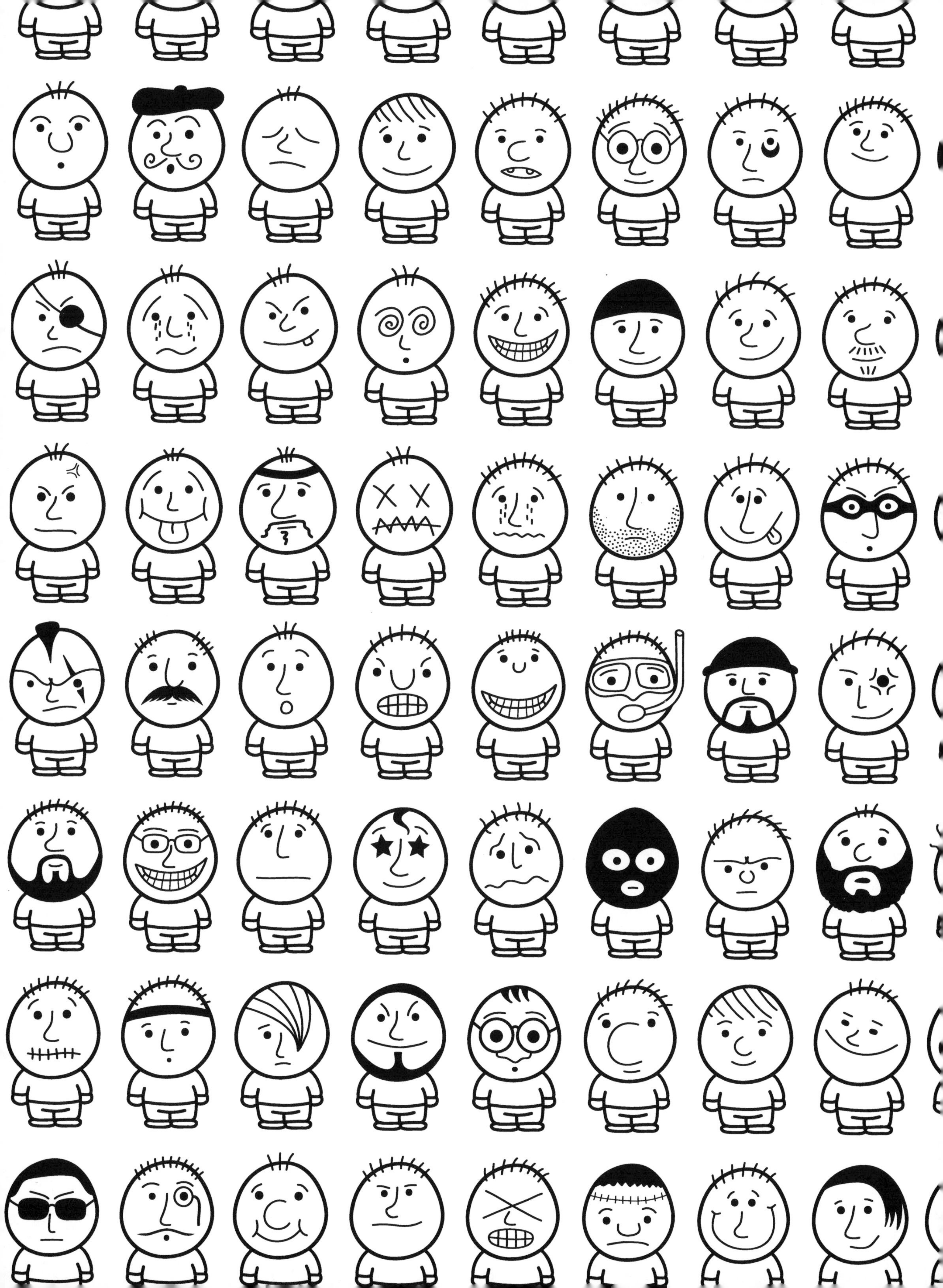

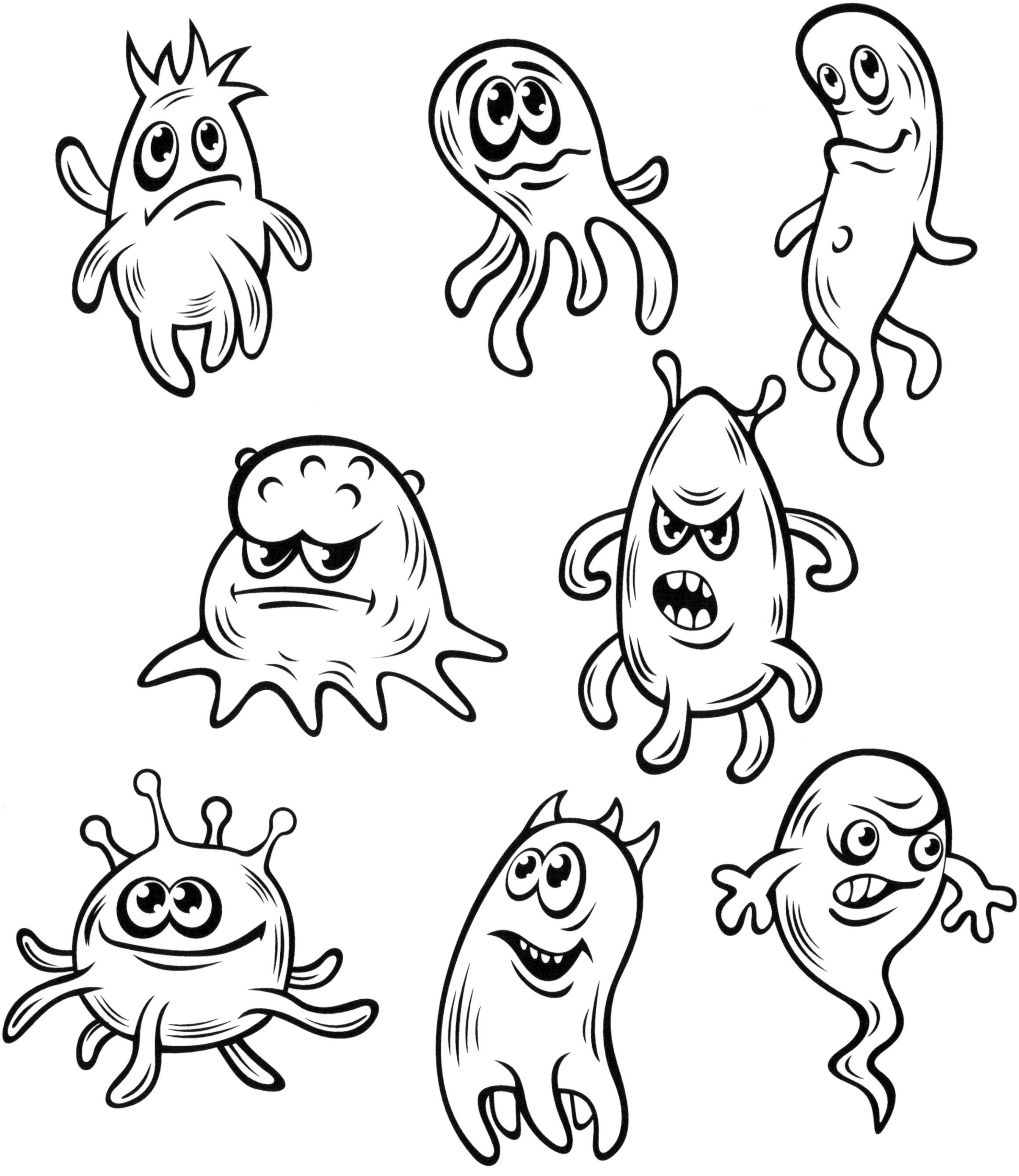

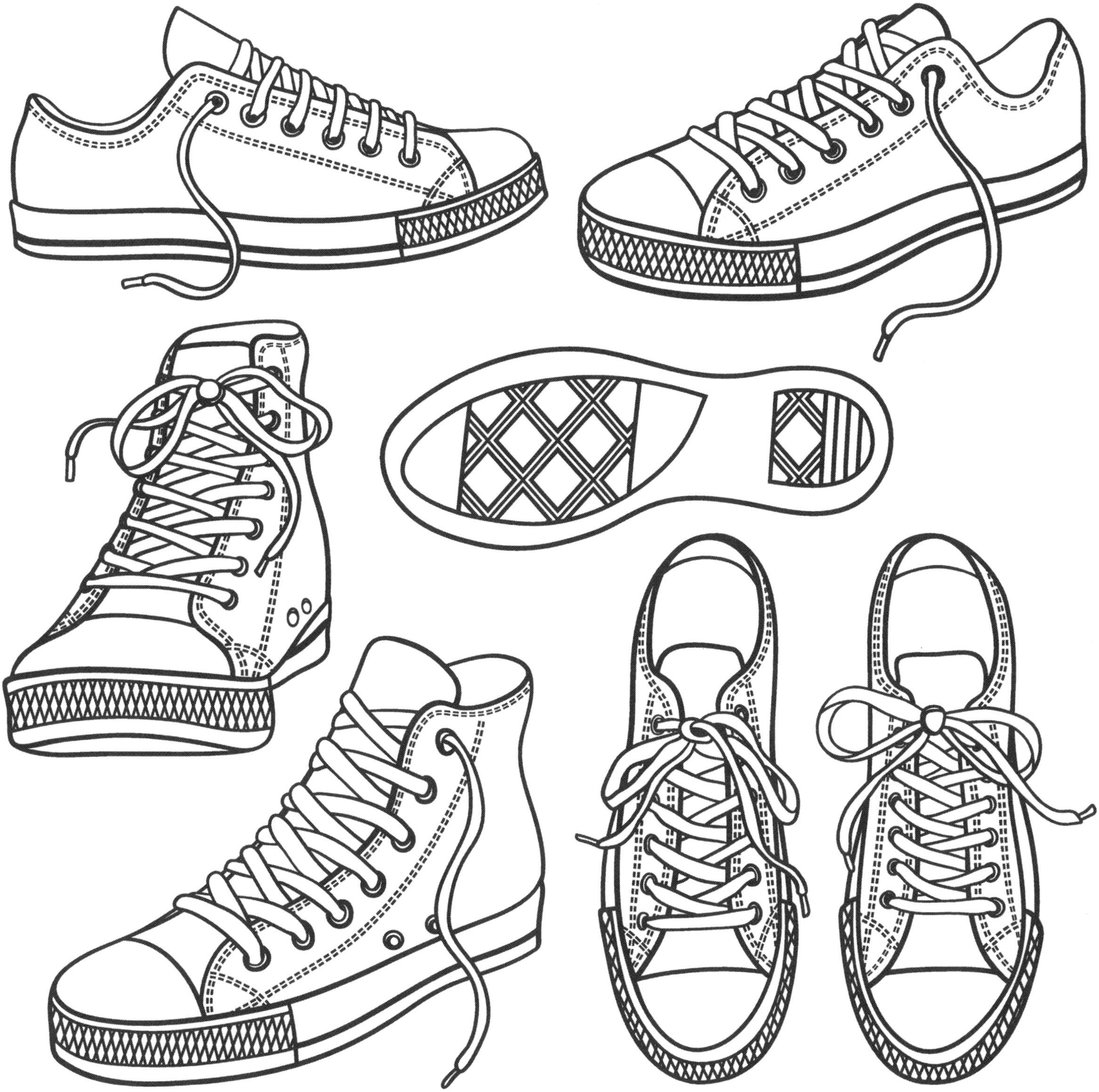

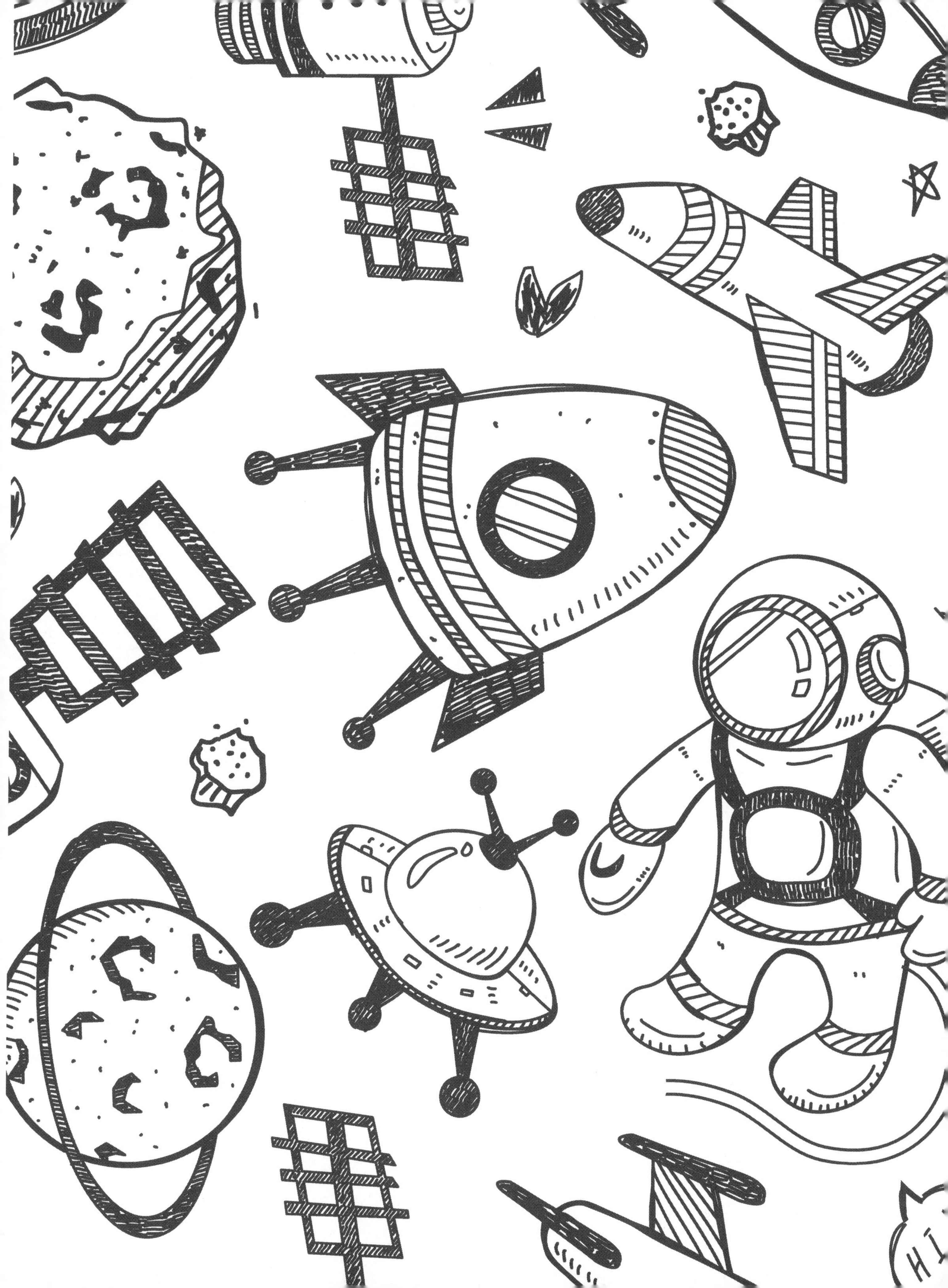
HI

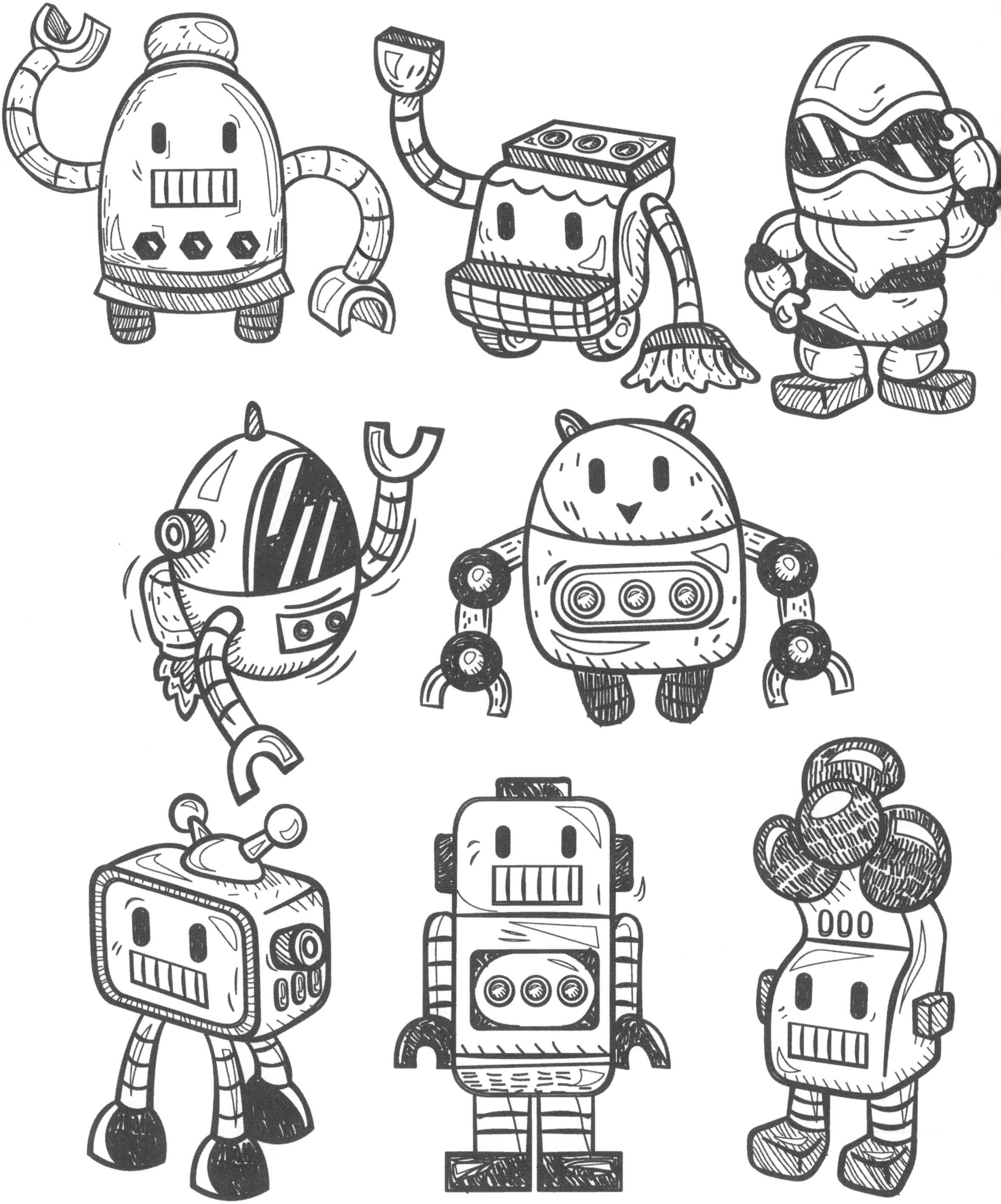

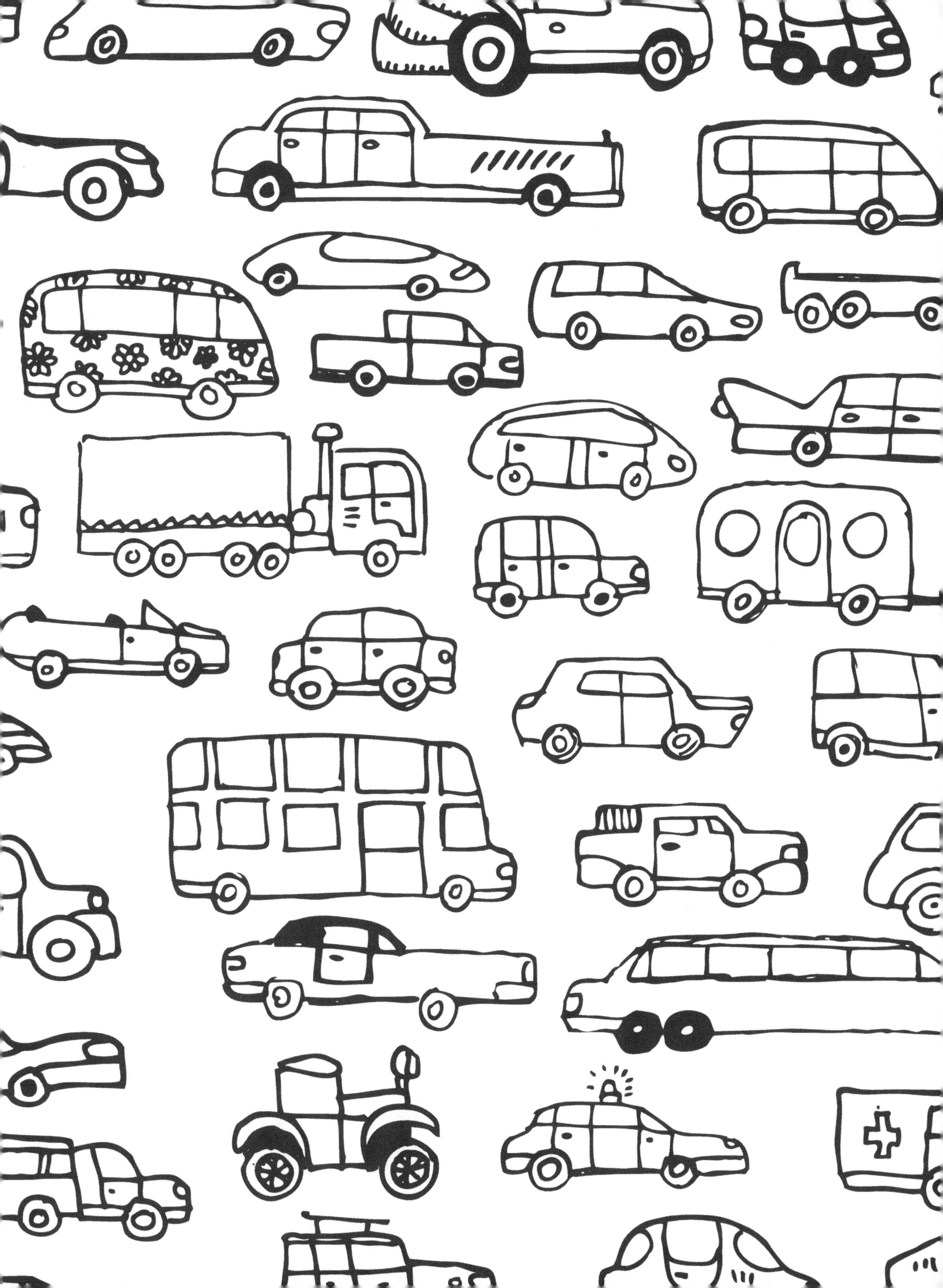

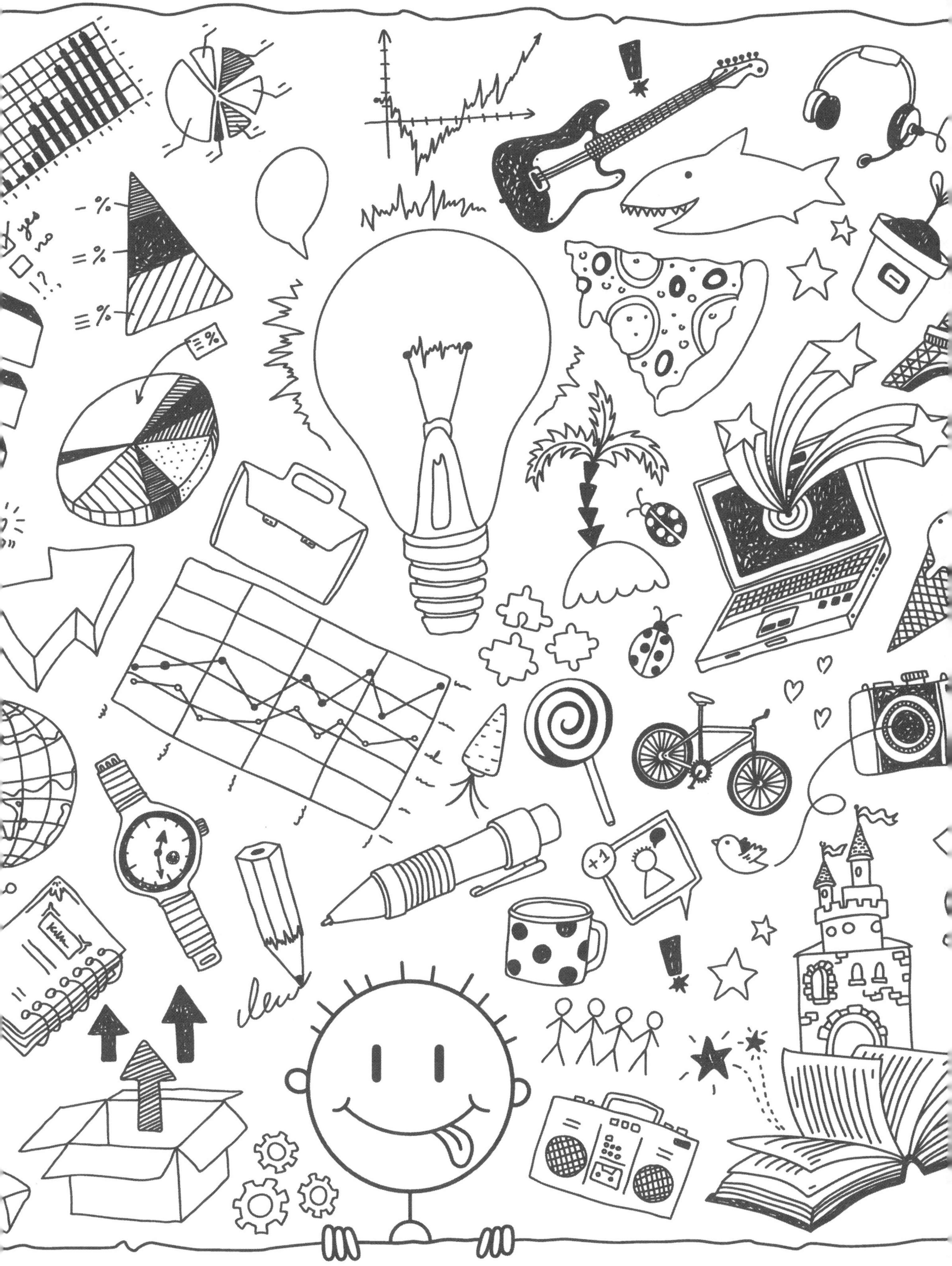
yes
no
+1

!
?
1
SCHOOL
A
D
B
C
$E = mc^2$
$\sqrt{x} = 4$
iDEA
$\pi = 3.14...$
2+2=4

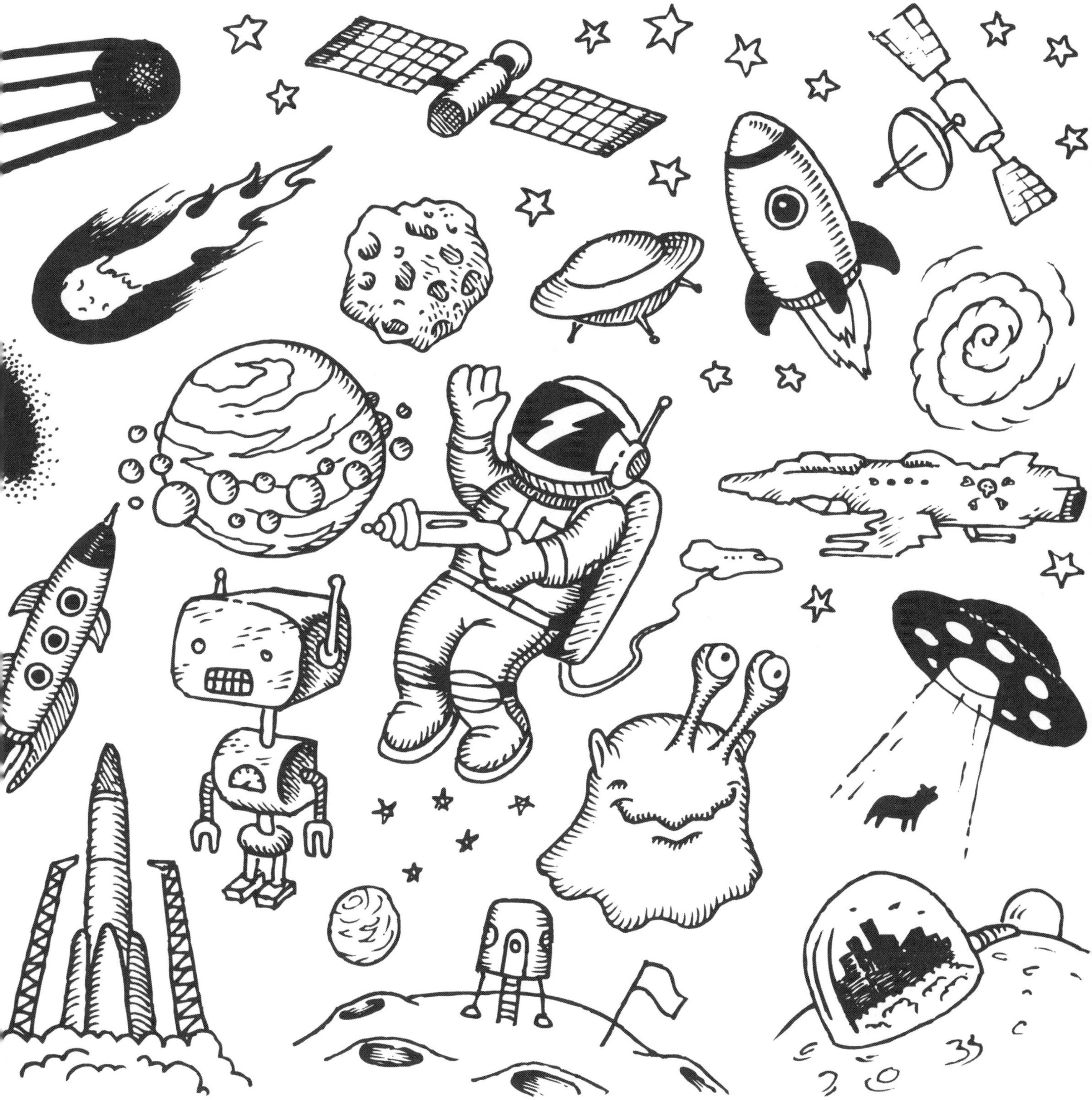

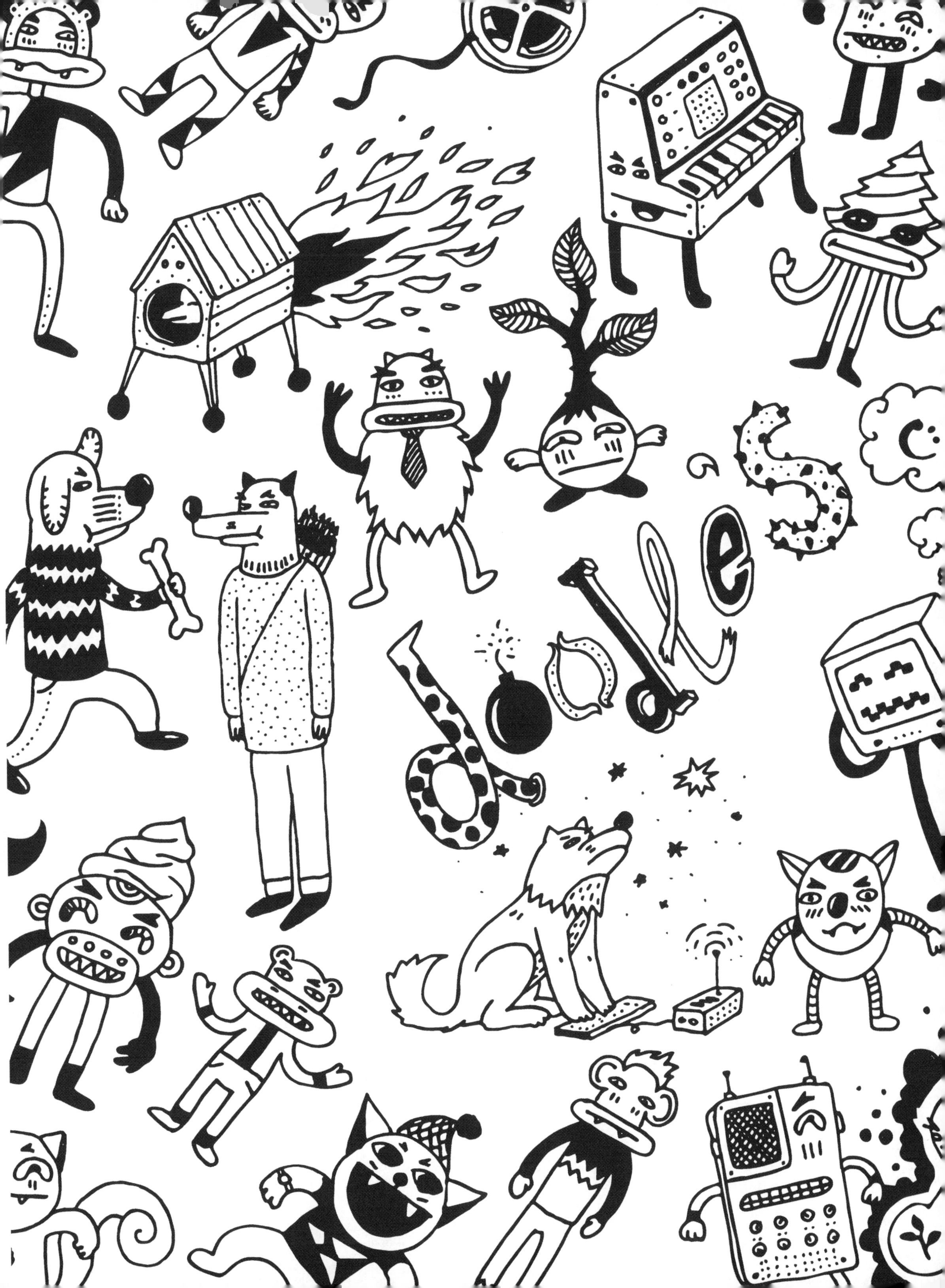
doodles

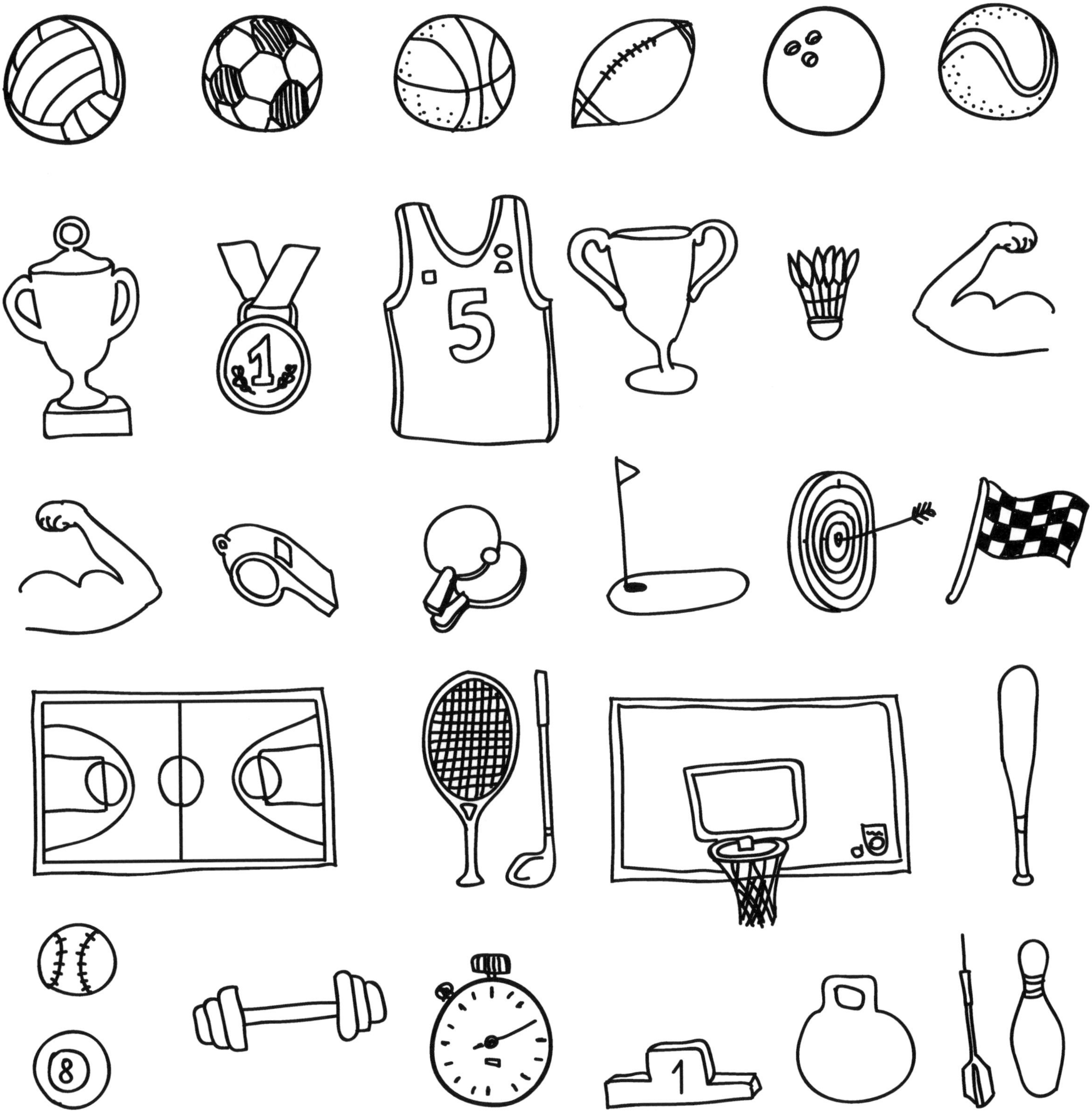
1
5
8
1

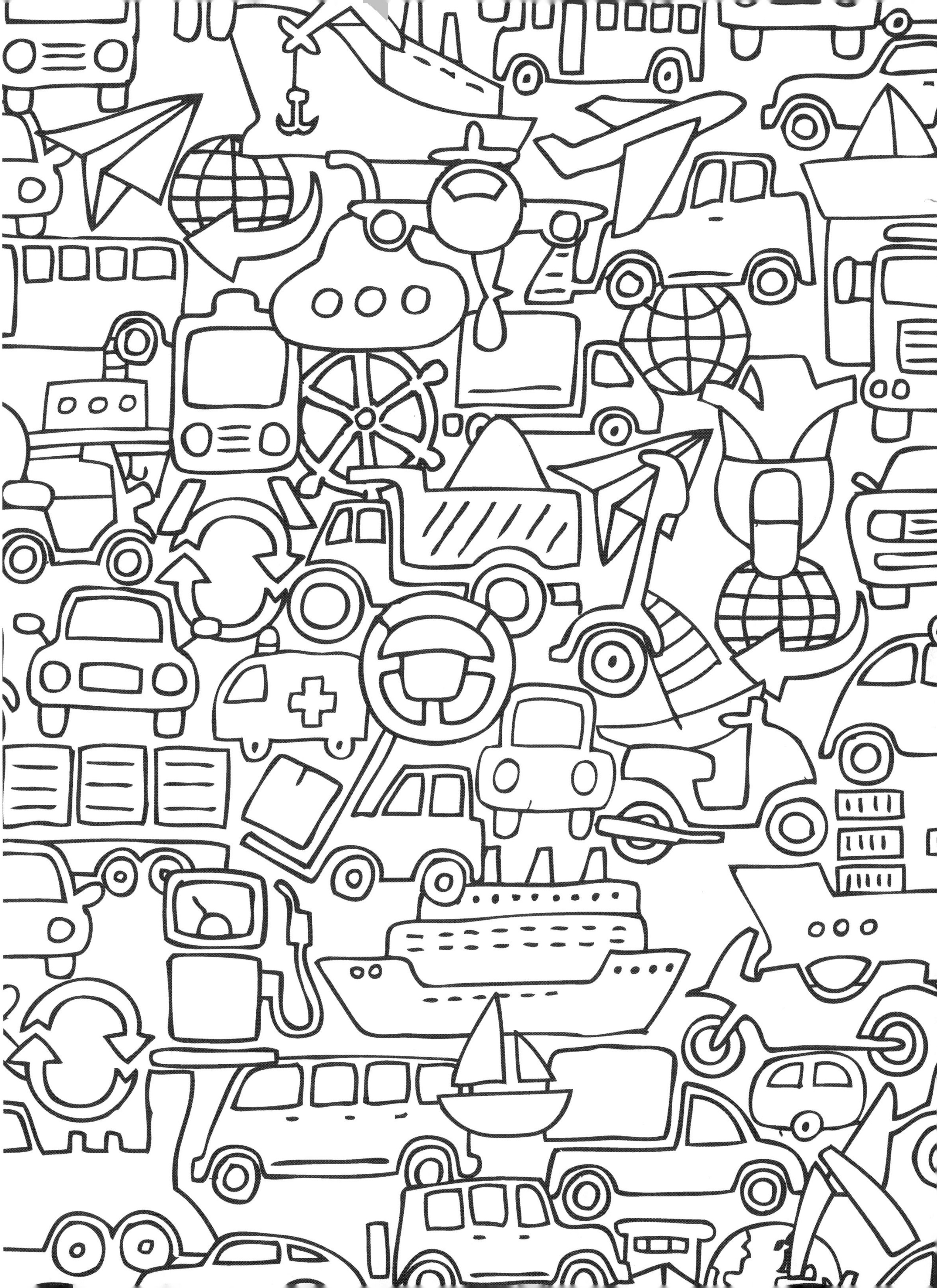

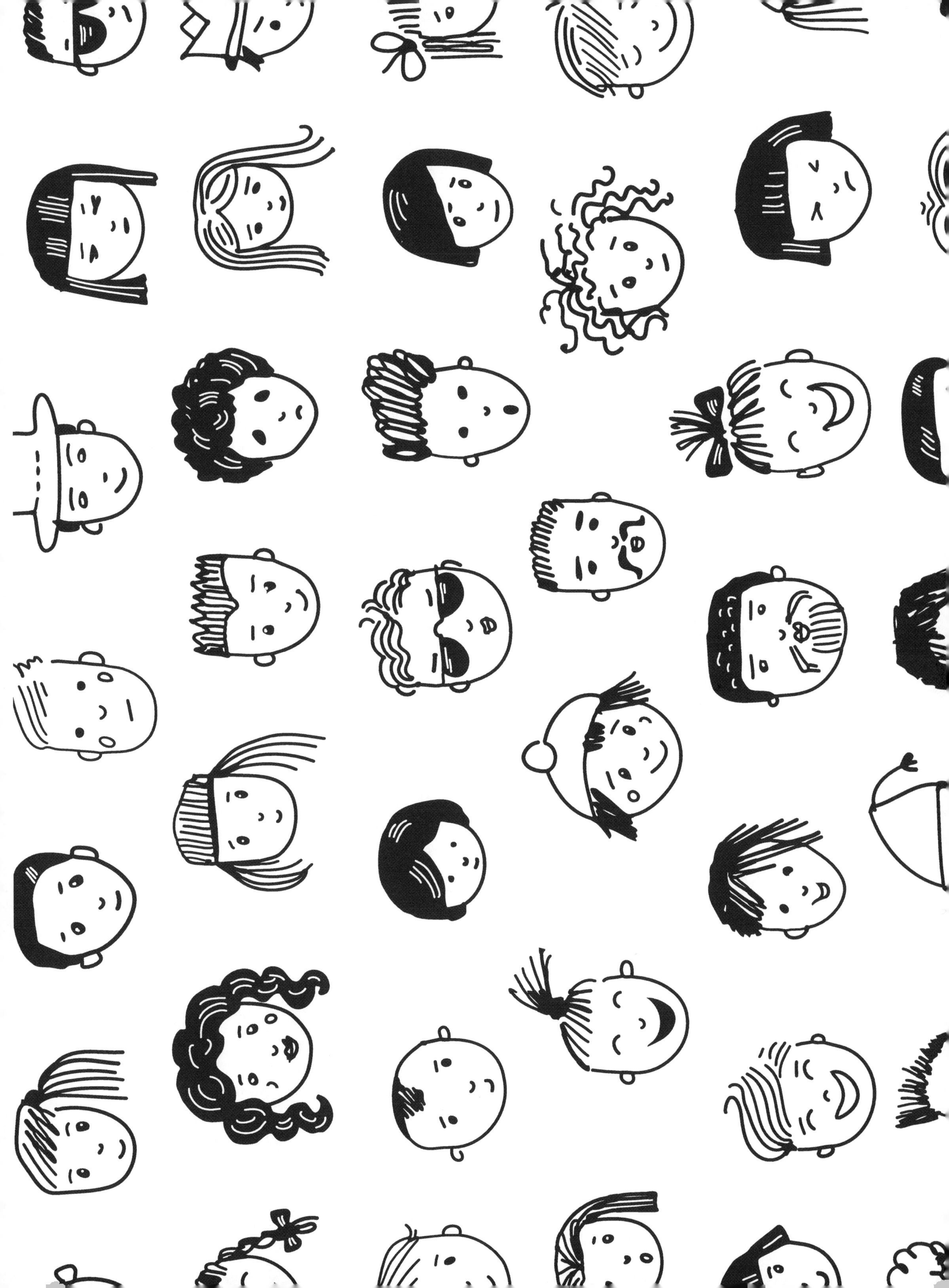

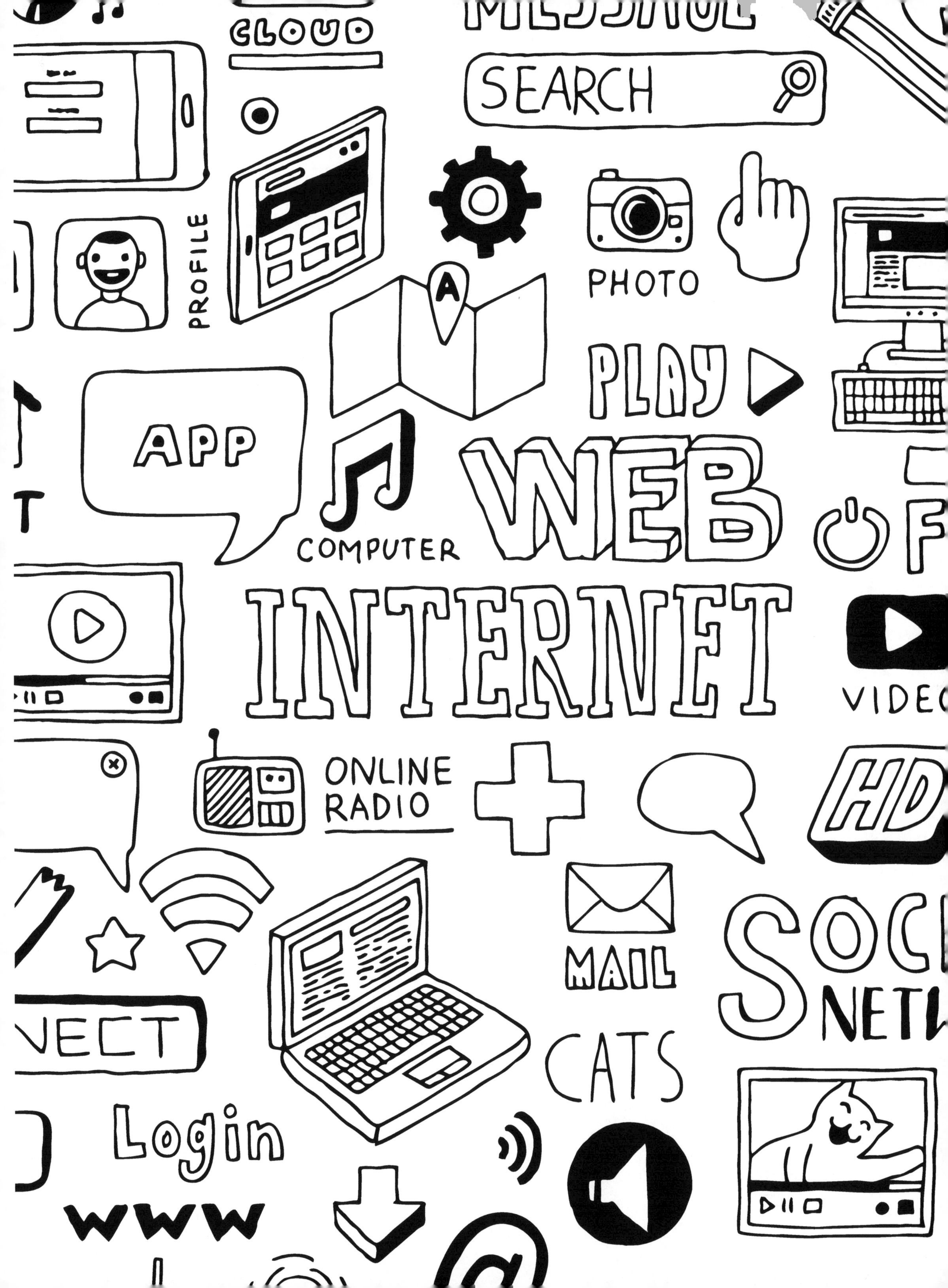
CLOUD
SEARCH
PROFILE
PHOTO
PLAY
APP
COMPUTER
WEB
INTERNET
ONLINE
RADIO
HD
MAIL
CATS
Login
WWW

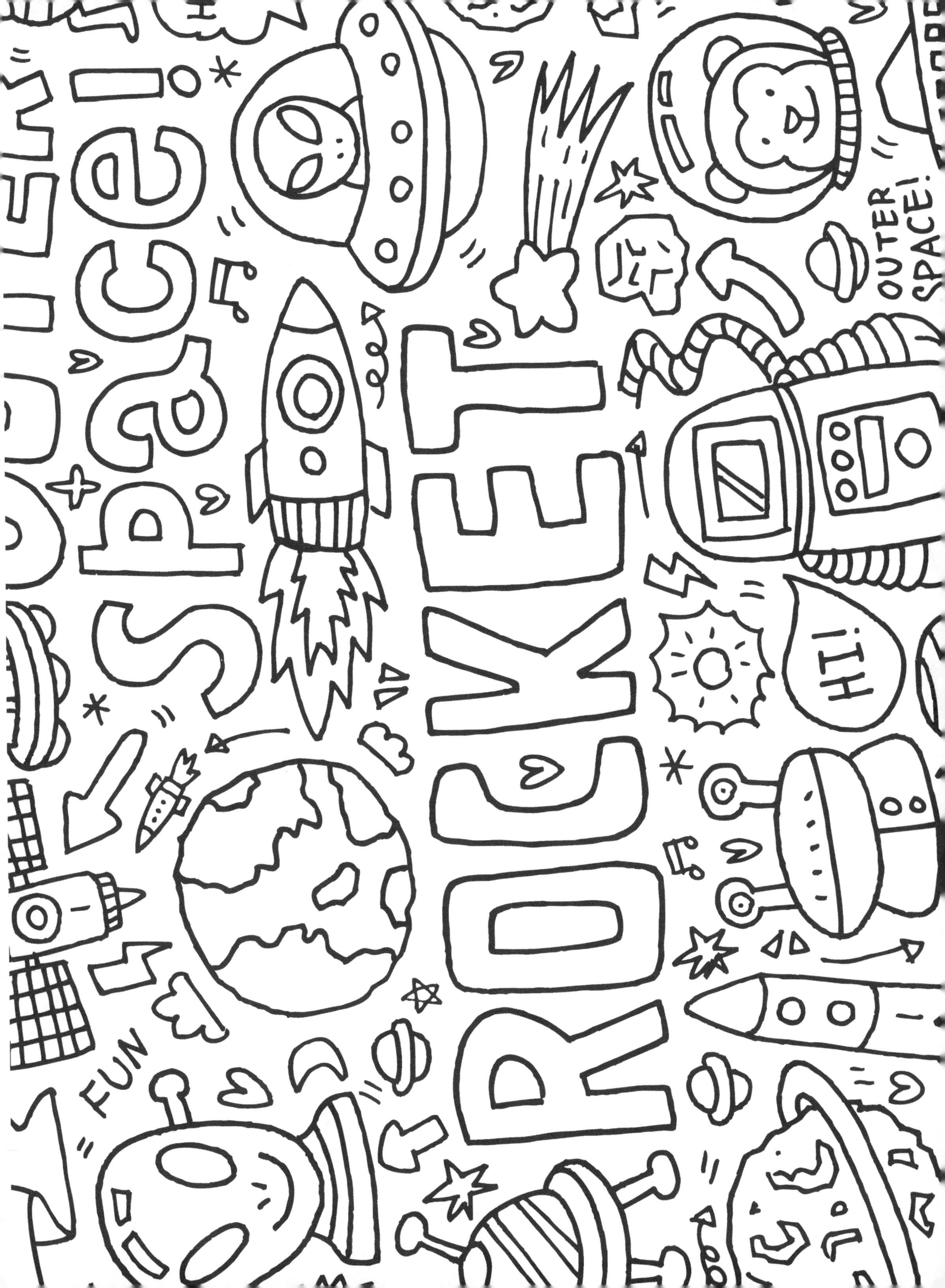

space
ROCKET
OUTER SPACE!
HI!
FUN

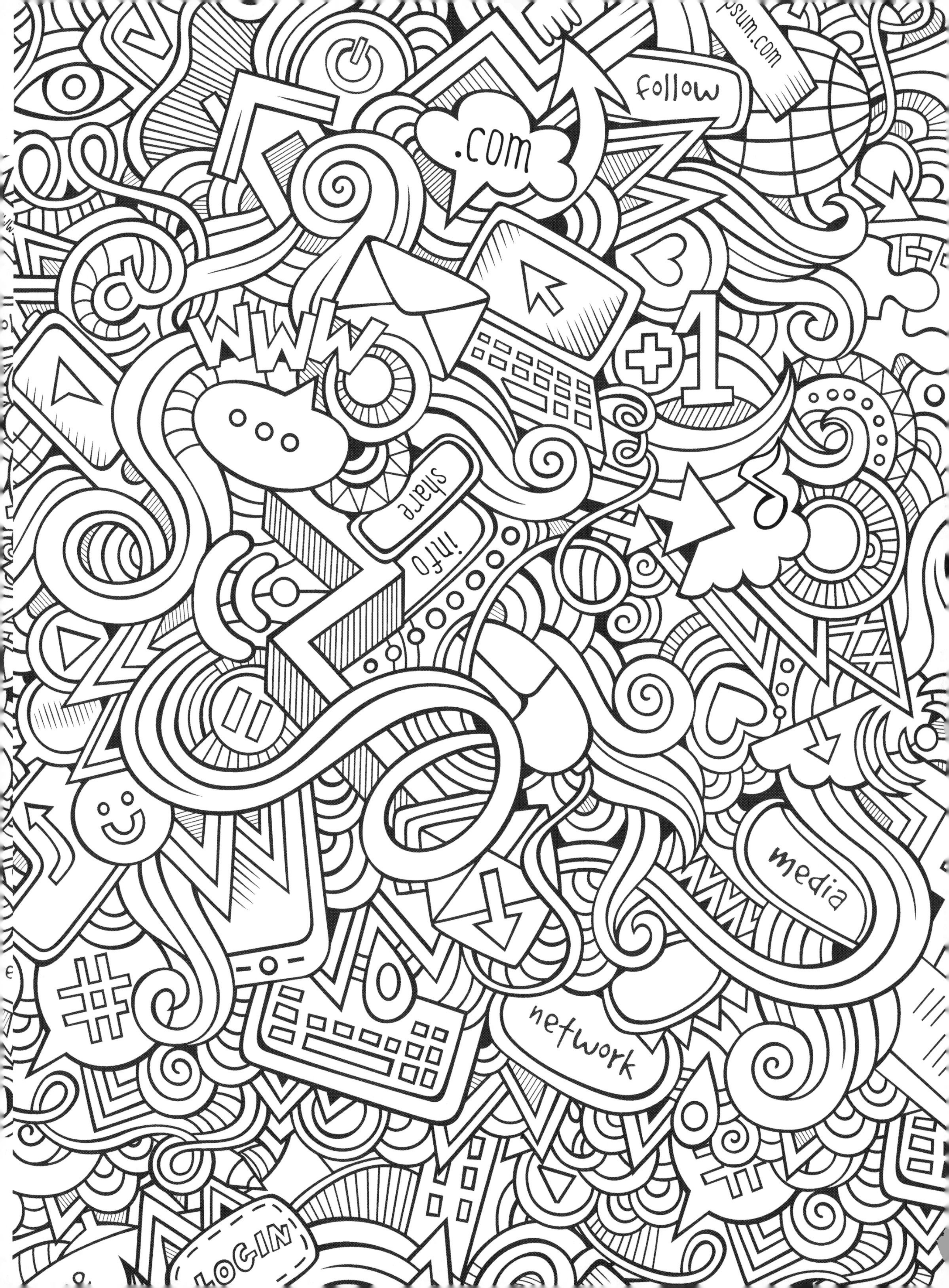
psum.com
follow
.com
www
+1
share
info
media
network
LOGIN

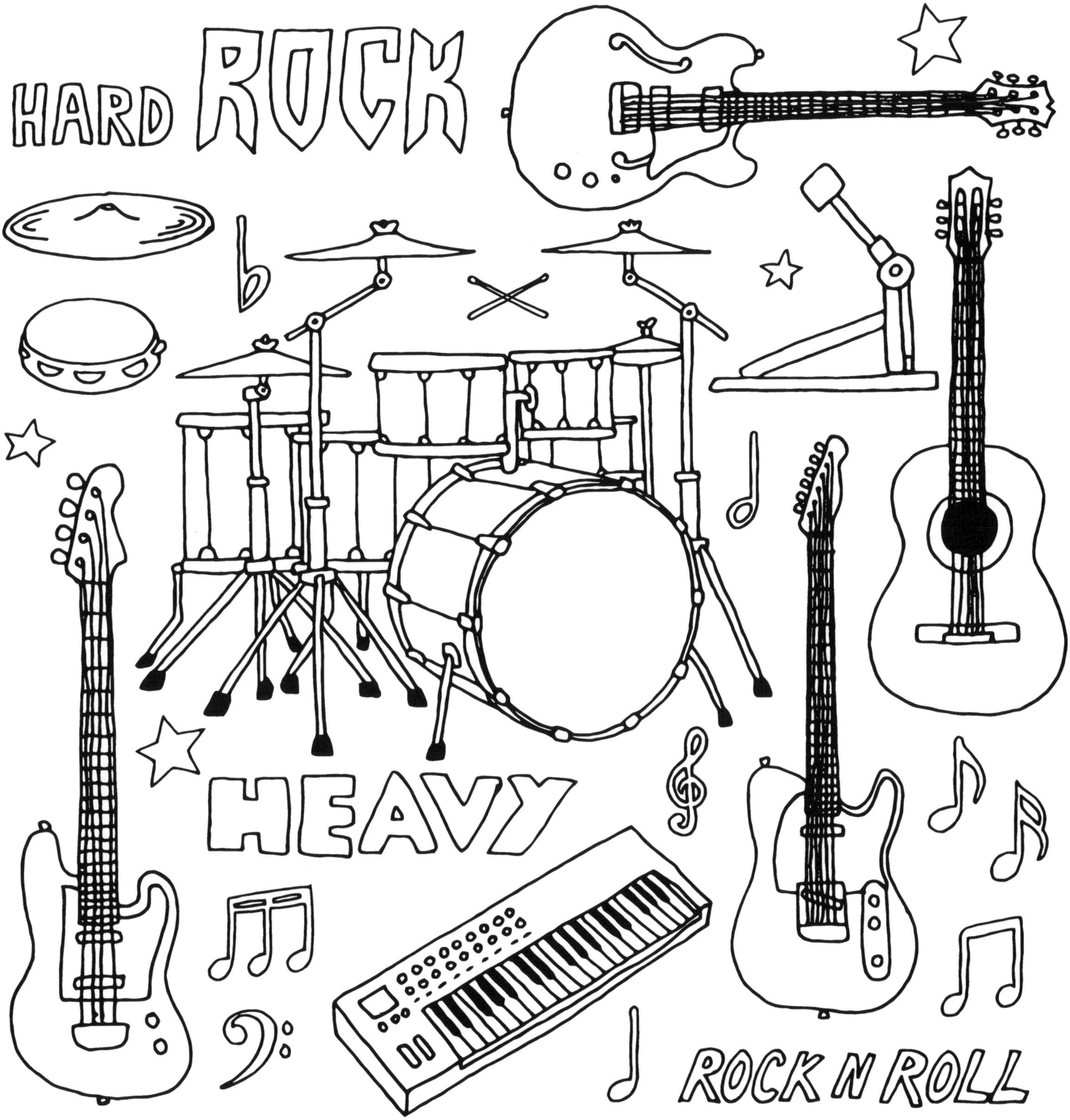
HARD ROCK
HEAVY
ROCK N ROLL

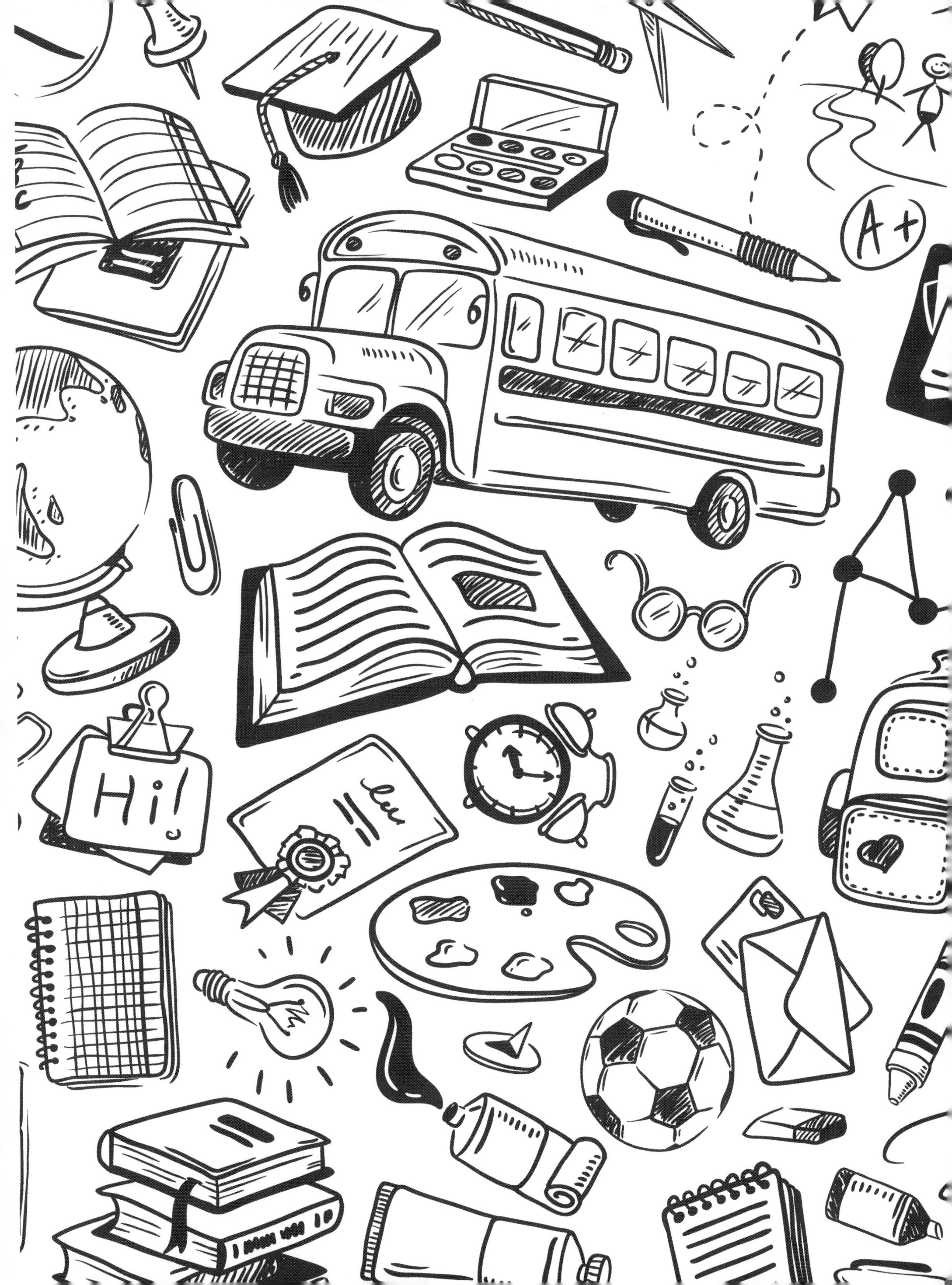
A+
Hi!

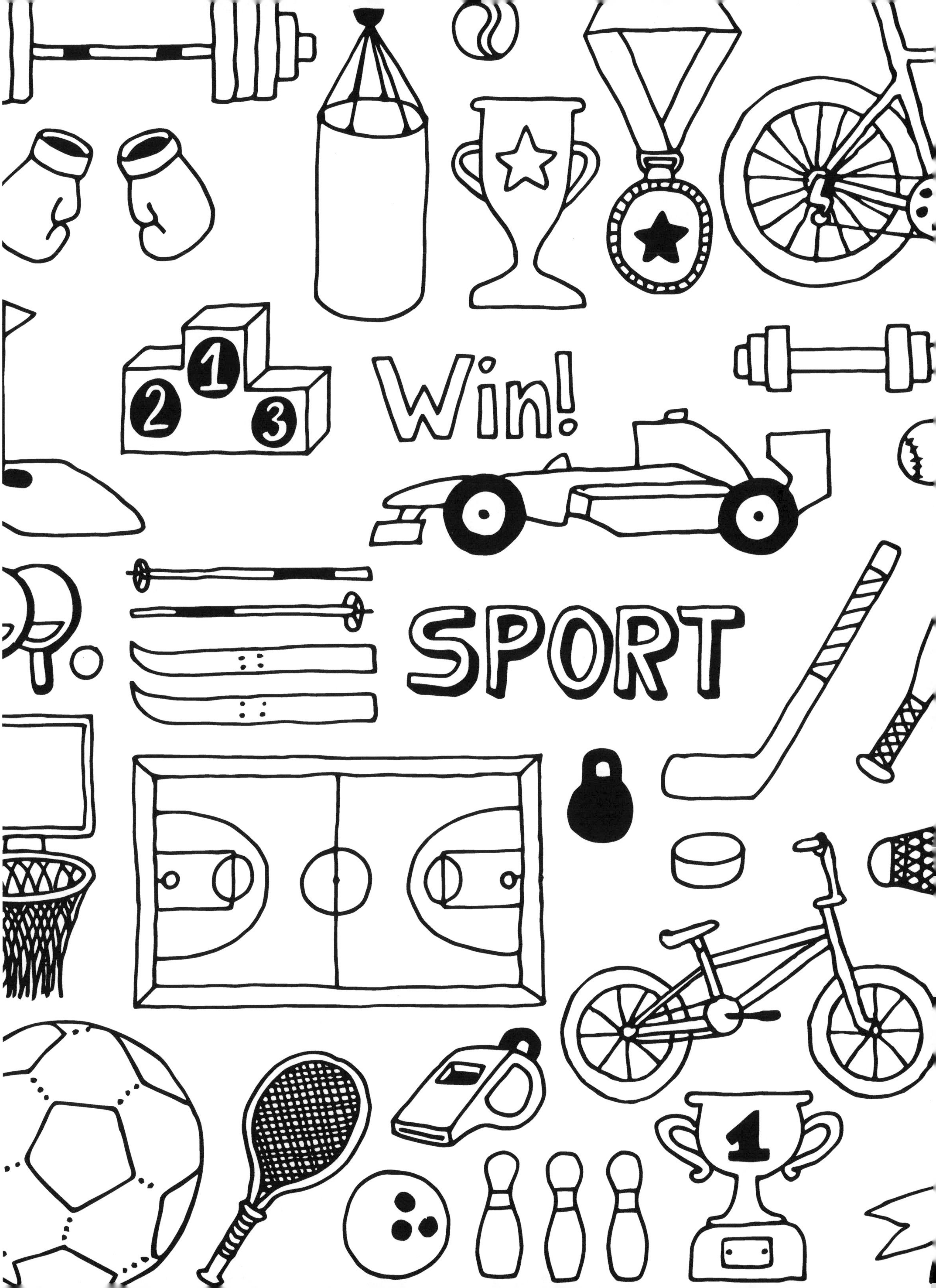
Win!
SPORT

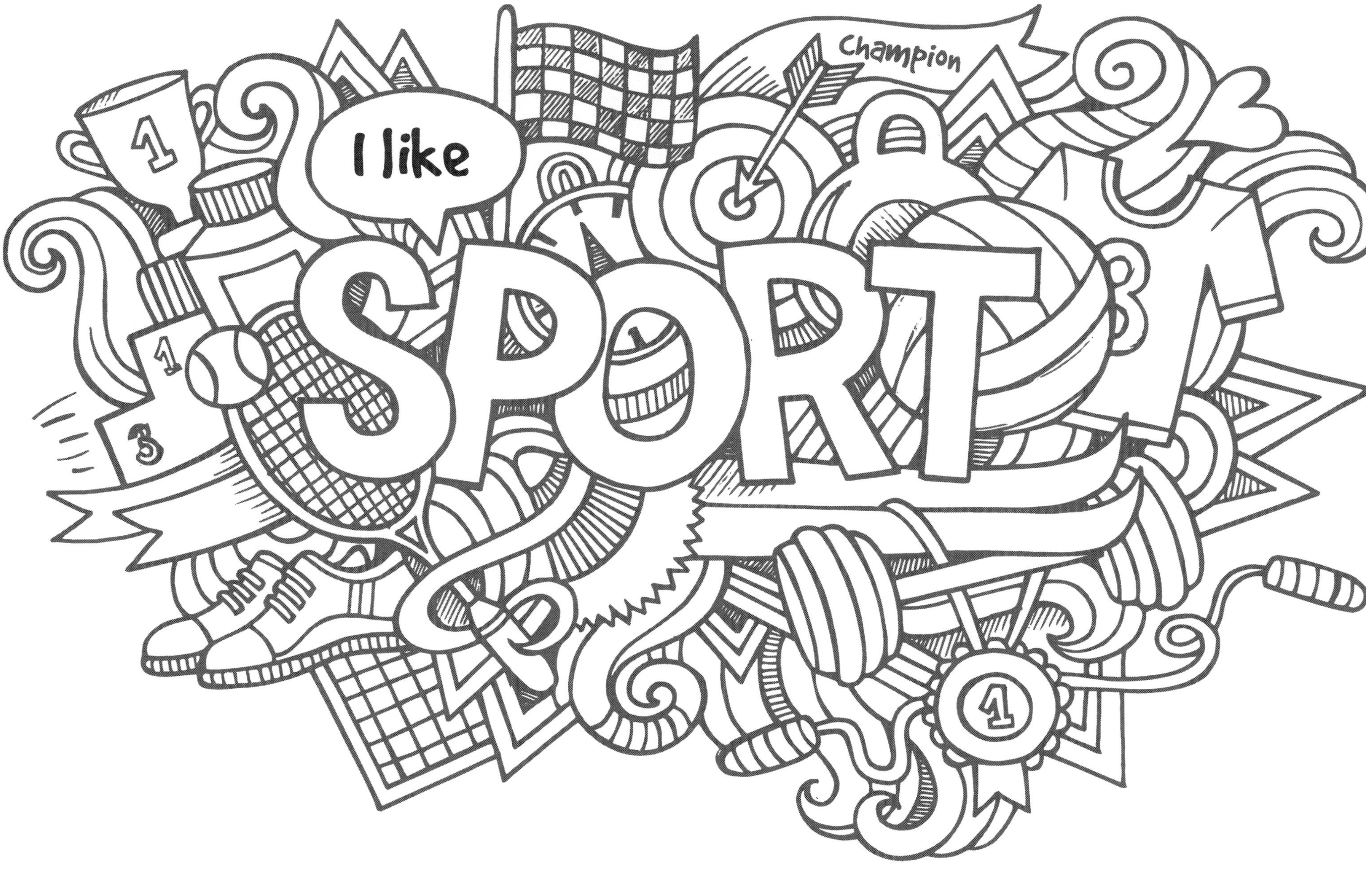

I like
SPORT
Champion

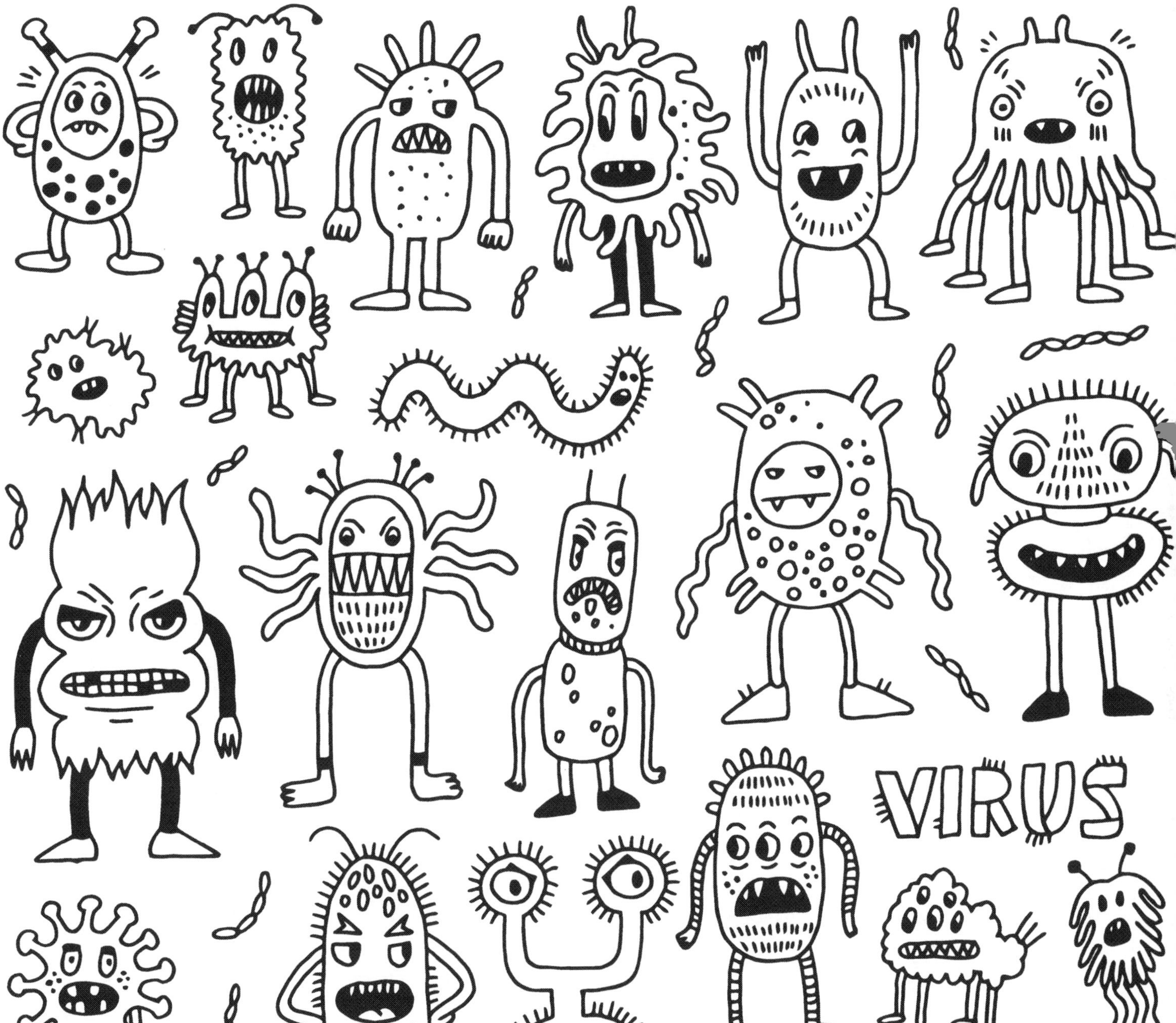
VIRUS

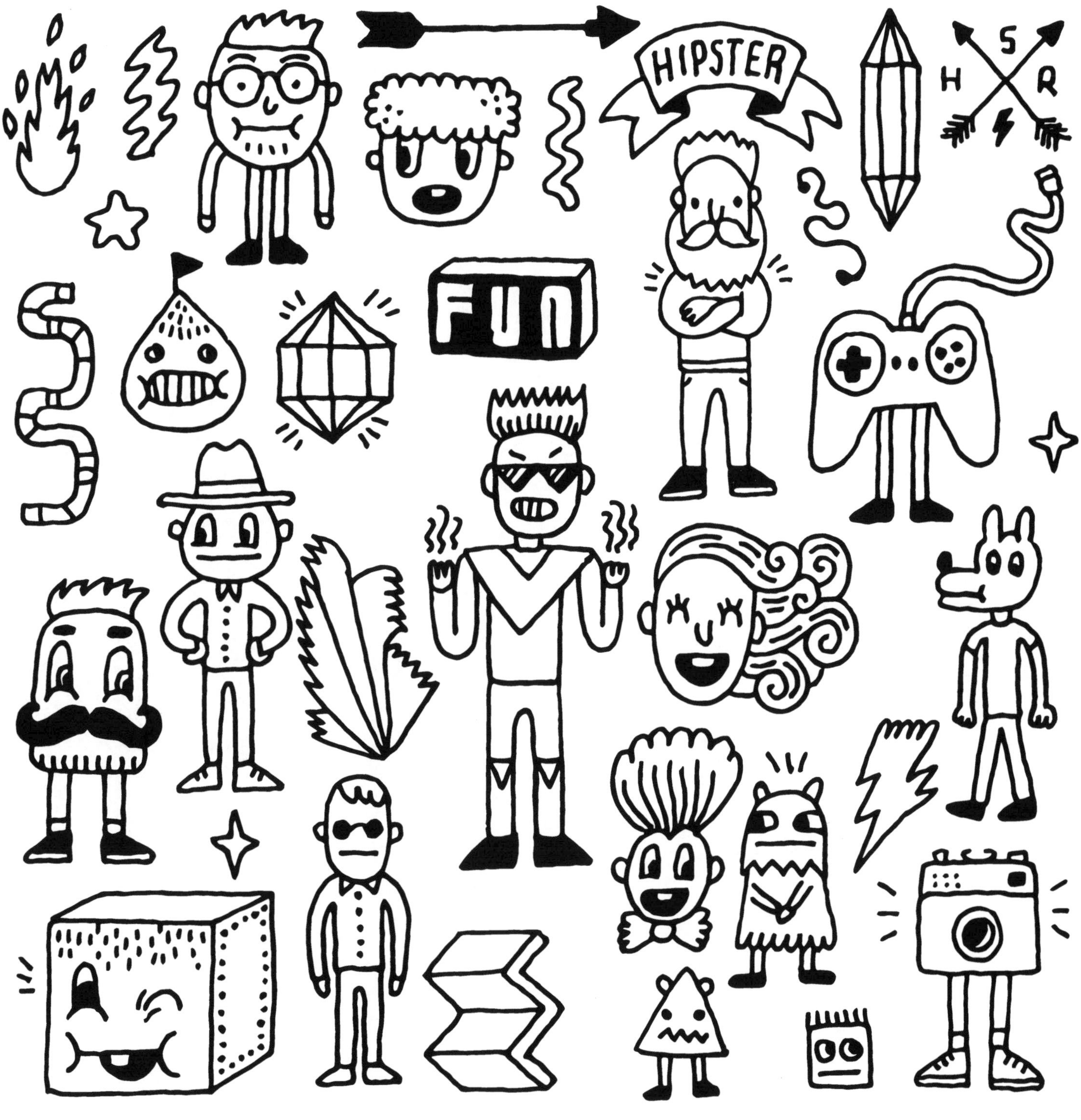
HIPSTER
H
S
R
FUN

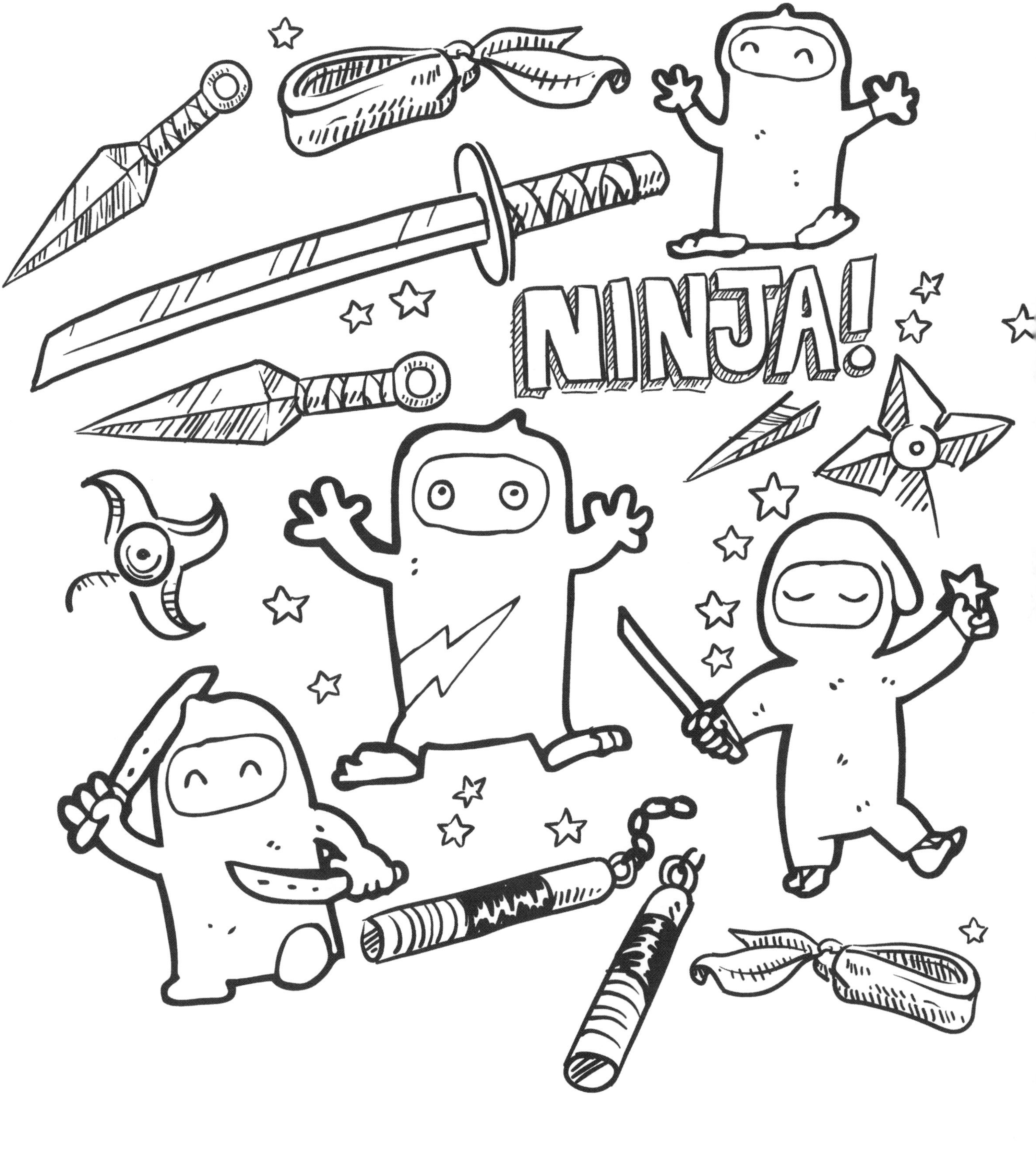
NINJA!